Chuckling Ducklings
and Baby Animal Friends

Aaron Zenz

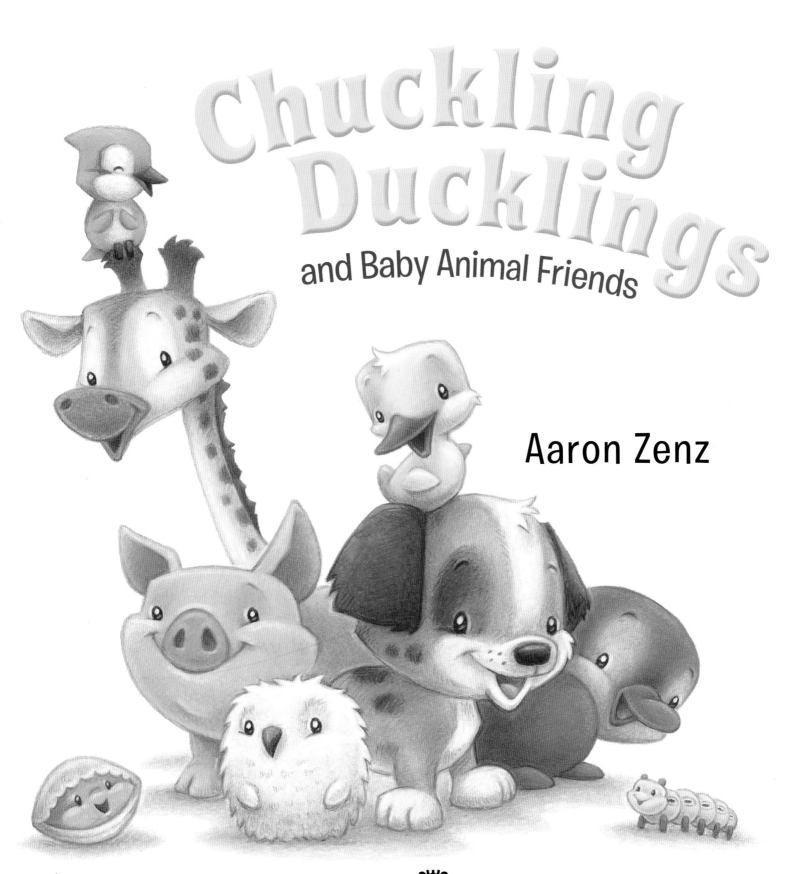

Walker & Company 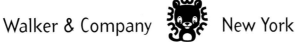 New York

Here's a **PUPPY**. There's a **KITTEN**.

A baby **BUNNY** is what I am.

A yawning **FAWN**

and chuckling **DUCKLINGS**.

CUB,

CUB,

CUB,

CUB,

PIGLET, LAMB.

He's a **COLT**

and she's a **FILLY**—

although both
are also
FOALS.

Butterflies were **CATERPILLARS**.

Frogs come from the wee **TADPOLES**.

OWLET,

CYGNET,

EAGLET,

EYAS,

GOSLING,

CHEEPER,

POULT, and

SQUAB.

As for all the rest of us birds,

CHICK will simply do the job.

PUGGLE? PUGGLE!

We're both **PUGGLES**.

KIT

and

PINKY,

PORCUPETTE.

What's a **CRIA**?

Who's a **JOEY**?

HATCHLINGS race the LEVERET.

CALVES of every shape, size, color.

I'm a **KID**. Are you one too?

PUP and **SPAT**,

WHELP and ELVER.

They call me small **FRY**.

How
about
you
?

BEAR
CUB

BLUE JAY
CHICK

BUTTERFLY
CATERPILLAR

CAMEL
CALF

DUCK
DUCKLING

EAGLE
EAGLET

ECHIDNA
PUGGLE

EEL
ELVER

ELEPHANT
CALF

GOAT
KID

GOOSE
GOSLING

HARE
LEVERET

HAWK
EYAS

MOUSE
PINKY

OSTRICH
CHICK

OTTER
WHELP

OWL
OWLET

OYSTER
SPAT

PIG
PIGLET

PIGEON
SQUAB

PLATYPUS
PUGGLE

PORCUPINE
PORCUPETTE

SHEEP
LAMB

SKUNK
KIT

SWAN
CYGNET

TIGER
CUB

TORTOISE
HATCHLING

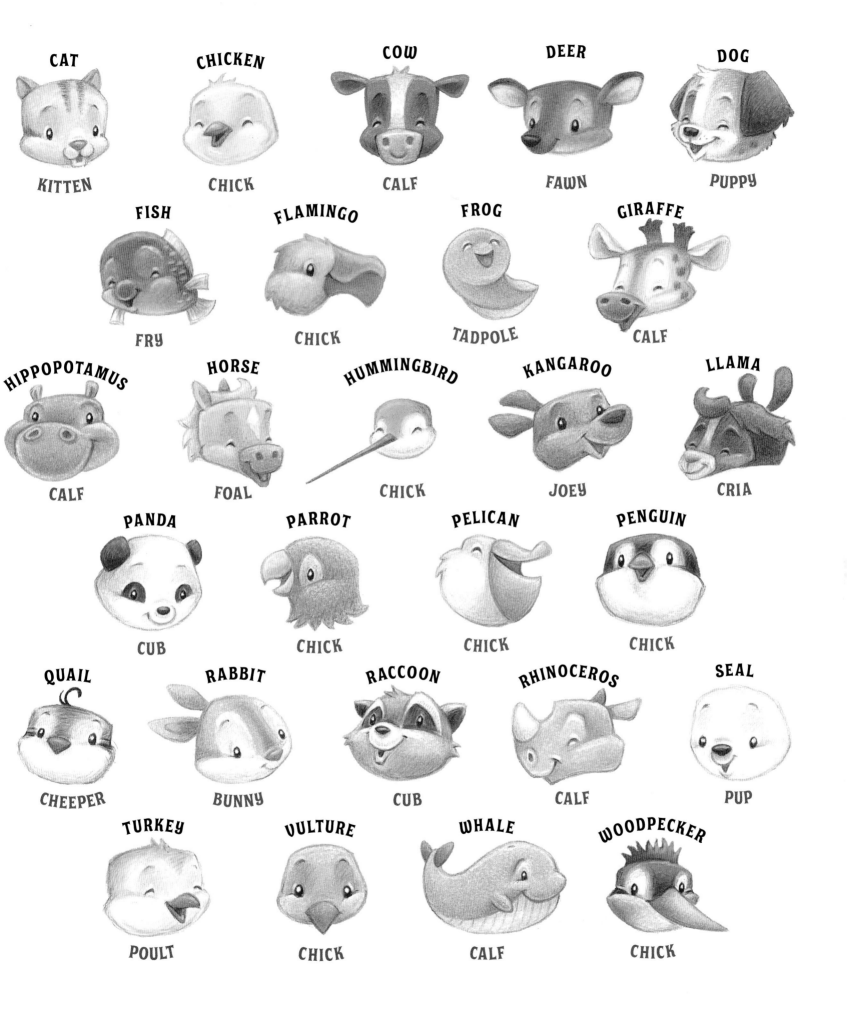

CAT
KITTEN

CHICKEN
CHICK

COW
CALF

DEER
FAWN

DOG
PUPPY

FISH
FRY

FLAMINGO
CHICK

FROG
TADPOLE

GIRAFFE
CALF

HIPPOPOTAMUS
CALF

HORSE
FOAL

HUMMINGBIRD
CHICK

KANGAROO
JOEY

LLAMA
CRIA

PANDA
CUB

PARROT
CHICK

PELICAN
CHICK

PENGUIN
CHICK

QUAIL
CHEEPER

RABBIT
BUNNY

RACCOON
CUB

RHINOCEROS
CALF

SEAL
PUP

TURKEY
POULT

VULTURE
CHICK

WHALE
CALF

WOODPECKER
CHICK

First published in the United States of America in February 2011
by Walker Publishing Company, Inc., a division of Bloomsbury Publishing, Inc.
www.bloomsburykids.com

For information about permission to reproduce selections from this book, write to
Permissions, Walker BFYR, 175 Fifth Avenue, New York, New York 10010

Library of Congress Cataloging-in-Publication Data
Zenz, Aaron.
Chuckling ducklings / Aaron Zenz.
p.   cm.
ISBN 978-0-8027-2191-4 (hardcover) · ISBN 978-0-8027-2192-1 (reinforced)
1. Animals—Infancy—Juvenile literature. I. Title.
QL763.Z46 2011   591.3'9—dc22   2010031649

Art created with colored pencils
Typeset in Arbitrary Regular and Shag Expert Exotica
Book design by Danielle Delaney

Printed in China by Toppan Leefung Printers, Ltd., Dongguan, Guangdong
1 3 5 7 9 10 8 6 4 2 (hardcover)
1 3 5 7 9 10 8 6 4 2 (reinforced)

All papers used by Bloomsbury Publishing, Inc., are natural, recyclable products
made from wood grown in well-managed forests. The manufacturing processes
conform to the environmental regulations of the country of origin.

For my duckling, **Lily**

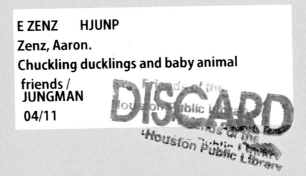